Miff and Joff

By Sascha Goddard

Miff is a cub.

Miff has lots of fluff.

Joff is a pup.

Joff has big fins.

Miff and Joff are pals.

Miff and Joff do fun stuff.

Miff and Joff get cod.

Miff scoffs it!

Joff nips it!

"Joff! I can run up
to the hill top," said Miff.

"Miff! I can get off the hill!"
said Joff.

"Will we get up on the cliff, Miff?" said Joff.

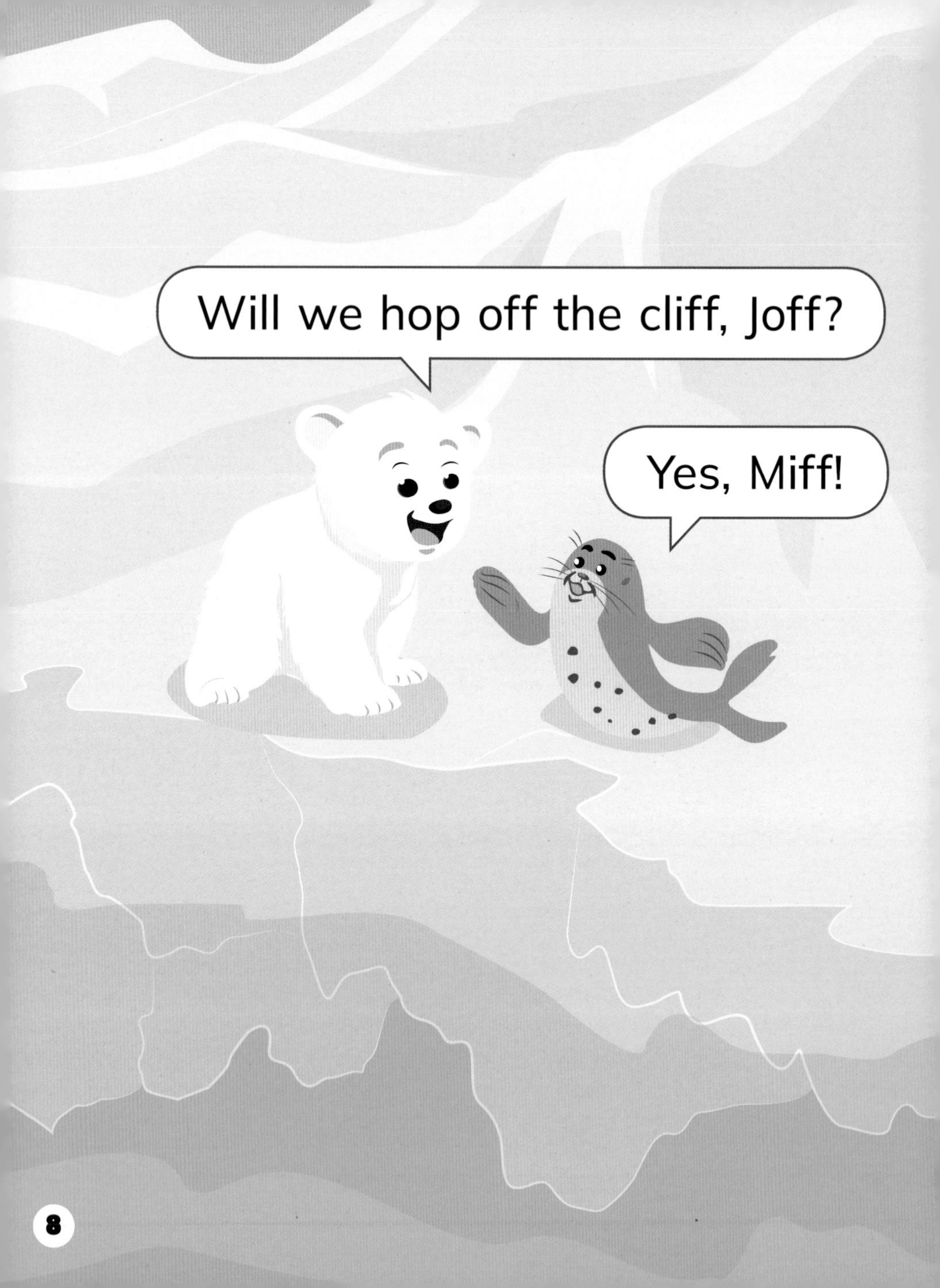
Will we hop off the cliff, Joff?
Yes, Miff!

"We do fun stuff, Joff!"
said Miff.

"We do, Miff!" said Joff.

CHECKING FOR MEANING

1. What do Miff and Joff eat? *(Literal)*

2. How does Joff get off the hill? *(Literal)*

3. How do you know Miff and Joff had fun? *(Inferential)*

EXTENDING VOCABULARY

fins	What are *fins*? What is another word that has a similar meaning? E.g. flippers. What do seals use their fins for?
scoffs	What is the meaning of *scoff*? What other words can you think of that mean to eat? E.g. bite, chew, gobble, munch, nibble.
huff and **puff**	What do *huff* and *puff* mean? Why did Miff and Joff huff and puff when they ran up the hill?

MOVING BEYOND THE TEXT

1. How do seals keep warm?

2. Why does Miff have lots of fluff? What types of covering do cubs have on their bodies? What other animals do you know that have fur?

3. Imagine a puppy and a kitten are pals. What might they do to have fun?

4. What are the cliffs made from in this story? Why?

SPEED SOUNDS

| ff | ll | ss | zz |

PRACTICE WORDS

fluff

Joff

Huff

Miff

stuff

hill

scoffs

puff

will

off

Will

cliff